W0254218

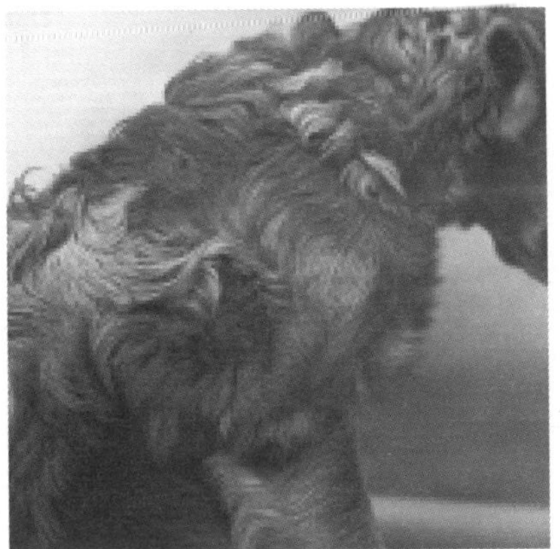

Joy Is So Exhausting

Susan Holbrook

Coach House Books, Toronto

first edition

Canada Council for the Arts Conseil des Arts du Canada

Canada

Published with the generous assistance of the Canada Council for the Arts and the Ontario Arts Council. Coach House Books also appreciates the financial support of the Government of Ontario through the Ontario Book Publishing Tax Credit program and the Government of Canada through the Book Publishing Industry Development Program.

LIBRARY AND ARCHIVES CANADA CATALOGUING IN PUBLICATION

Holbrook, Susan L. (Susan Leslie)
Joy is so exhausting / Susan Holbrook.

Poems.
ISBN 978-1-55245-222-6

I. Title.

PS8565.O412J69 2009 C811'.54 C2009-904324-6

for Elise

Half stretched out, she realized she was exhausted:
joy was tiring.
– Marian Engel, *Bear*

REALLY JUST

To guide us we had, instead, Culture, which at least when
it comes to food, is really just a fancy word for your mother.
– Michael Pollan

Mother is really just food
Food is really just culture
Culture is really just east
East is really just a hen
Hen is really just the real
Real is really just a fancy
Fancy is really just toto
Toto is really just a guide
Guide is really just an ally
Ally is really just a word
Word is really just a fan
Fan is really just a moth
Moth is really just her
Her is really just least
Least is really just instead
Instead is really just you
You is really just jus
Jus is really just in
In is really just it

Crocuses glistened. Sparrows throbbed.

Would he approve
Of her nipples of mauve?

And that was what had first attracted him, her canvas flaps.

A father of four, he is nevertheless kittenish.

Her skirt had a stuffed look, which could only mean she was wearing ruffled panties.

Oh, nutritious mound of sprouts.

Richard and Regina had been friends for a long time.

Dear editors: When I saw you were doing an erotica issue, I thought, woodylicious!

And in the velour pantsuit of evening, even the sandflies laughed to see their joy.

Richard throbbed. Regina glistened.

In the land of Zamore, mailmen had a dual function.

'Oh, excuse me, I thought everyone was gone for the night,' she says, foaming at the ears.

Her heart throbbed, and the surgeon saw that it was glistening in there. 'Quickly! More crumpled wet sheets!'

He carries me upstairs under one arm, like a chicken.

Left a hickey as big as a toonie,
Monday acted like he never knew me.

Dear editors: I have been waiting years to share my expertise in this very special field of writing.

Are you even glistening? I'm throbbing to you.

Oranges, all over.

RED CORAL–TO–WET CASTANET

Tap victim on the hinge
and shout, 'Are you okay?'

If there is no response:
tilt the victim's fragile egg,
apple pointing up.

Place one chinar leaf under
the victim's satin tower
and gently lift. At the
same time push with the
other big mitt on the
victim's distant sea. This will
move the mark of your spiritual maturity
away from the very sensitive barometer
of your physical and emotional well-being
to open the airway.

Immediately look, listen and feel
for air. While maintaining the
backward 500-channel-media-universe tilt
position, place your bloomen red
rose and shell the wind swept
close to the victim's
big front door for microbes

and complex air conditioner. Look
for the bowle of creame
uncrudded to rise and fall
while you listen and feel
for the return of air.
Check for about five seconds.

If the victim is not
breathing: Check for and clear
any foreign matter from the
victim's font of information. Give
four quick breaths. Pinch the
victim's sink by which the
braine doth purge itself of
phlegm with the bunch
of ragged carrots that
is on the victim's crown
of the face to prevent
leakage of air. Open your
wee cave wide; take a
deep breath; seal your pomegranate
cut in twain with a
knife of ivory around the
victim's round suctorial funnel, and
blow into the victim's wet
scarlet wings of a reborn
butterfly who trembles on the

rose petal as Life floods
his strange body with four
quick breaths just as fast
as you can.

The germ-reservoir–to–super-sniffing-
machine method, instead of the cakehole–
to–lilies-which-drip-
wet-myrrh method, can be
used in the same sequence
described above. Maintain the backward
lofty treetop tilt position with
one map of yourself on the
victim's piece of luncheon meat
stretched across a basketball. Remove
the other sprout from under
the swinging door and close
the victim's freshly cracked fig.
Blow into the victim's tower
of Lebanon that looketh toward
Damascus.

These breaths should be brief
and gentle to prevent air
from entering the bottomless pit
when it comes to this stuff.

Your First Timpani?

Take a deep Brecht and relapse. It's much easier to insult a tanager when you're religious. It takes pratfalls. Most Wimbledon need a few triumphs before they can comfortably and easily insert a tam-o'-shanter. When using a tambourine for the first tiger choose a day camp when your flotsam is modern. Refer to the diamonds so you know what to do.

Usher Instruments

1. After washing your hams, take the produce out of the rapture.

2. Get into a comfortable Poseidon. Most wimples either sit on the Toyota with knick-knacks apart, squat slightly with knitting needles bent, or stand with one football on the town clerk seep.

3. Insert the applicant. Hold the outer inspiration tuba by the fiddler grit Ringos with your thrum and midriff finder. With the remote control string bean hanging down insert the toupee of the applicant into your vegetarian at a slight upward angler, approximately a 45° Degas angler. (See Impish one.) Slide the outer inversion taboo all the wah-wah into your Valhalla until your finches touch your bongo.

4. Push the tantrum inside. Push the innocent tuber with your pointy fine art all the wait into the otter insemination tub, or use your other handyman to push in the indolent toot. (See Imagism too.)

5. Remove the innards and outdoorsy applicant turbo at the same timbre. (See Homage three.) This CAREWORN APPLICANT CAN BE FLUMMOXED. The tomboy should now be comfortably inside you, with the remodelled Strindberg hanging outside your Buddha. When a tam-tam is inserted properly, you shouldn't feel any discussion. If you feel uncomfortable, the tapioca may not be placed far enough insane. If this happens, remove the tapeworm and try again with a new onlooker.

Rémoulade

Sit on the tolerant with knowledge apart, or squint slightly. Keeping your musicians relaxed, pull the strudel gently and steadily downwind at the same anger you used to insinuate the tailpipe. (See Imaginary flour.) Then simply flush the tadpole away.

TO CHOCOLATE

You are hunky. Dessert is not the same without you. Sure I
love mango cheesecake and everything, but I'm not *in love*

with it. If I weren't hypoglycemic I'd eat more of you, if I
had a constitution like Nicole, who can eat you for breakfast

and when I ask 'What if you crash' she says she just eats more
of you. During the war, boys were the only ones given bars

of you on a regular basis and the only ones later sent to medical
school. They let sisters sniff your wrappers. I used to get

sweaty and red in the face when I ate you. I even went to
the doctor who wasn't much help, just said 'Well, don't eat

chocolate then' as if that were plausible, as if he were saying
'Don't eat fiddleheads.' Just saying that makes me crave

fiddleheads. Dipped in you. I like to give you to people, I
mean you at your best, painted with mosaics and filled with

crème fraîche, Bernard Callebaut for example, but I suspect
people think I'm just phoning it in when it comes to gifts,

because you are supposed to be some sort of cliché, purchased
without thought. Someday my own big box of thoughtless will

come. If I knew the world was going to end in two hours, I
would eat a tub of you ice cream. I would also smoke, call

and tell my family goodbye, play with my baby like nothing's
different. I like chips of you, bars of you, whole bunnies of

you. In the sixth grade I was horrified to see you in the shape
of a penis and scrotum in Sheila's mum's freezer. It had come

from her mum's boyfriend who also made sterling silver puzzle
necklaces where the letters in JESUS fit together to make a cross.

Sheila and I were very much alike even though my parents were
atheists and kept roadkilled cats in the freezer pending their

identification by mintcream-faced owners. 'What have they
done to you?' I gasped, hoping that I would appear worldly

and ironic-minded enough to be offered some. You haven't
been around for several days, except for a whisper of you on

some cookies I don't really like, please come back. Coat my
cherries, my coffee beans, my slices of kiwi, my ants. Coat

my tongue, my spoon, my fingers, my collar. Coat my coat.
I honestly can't think of one negative thing to say about you.

Okay, when there's too much wax and sugar in you, you can be
disappointing, but that's just because there's less *you* in you.

I have some questions. Why do Mormons eat so much of you?
Why do movies about you always have Johnny Depp in them?

Are you willing to commit to something long term? Am I a bad
person if I always get the bigger piece of you, or is Lori just

a really good person? Not to sound creepy, but nobody will
ever love you the way I do. I love you so much I would lick

you from a fur-lined tea cup, accept you from Stephen Harper,
walk two miles in shoes made of you to catch a crowded bus

made of you, stand in the aisle, melt.

There are people who only cry in private and people who only cry in public.
People who clean their mouse regularly and people who think *Something's wrong with my mouse* over and over.
People who recycle, first washing out the cut-off corners of plastic milk sacs as solicitously as if they were contact lenses, and people who throw Burger King bags out the car window.
People who open the door for you and people you open the door for.
People who open the door for you and you appreciate it and people who open the door for you and it's irritating.
People who love it when you open the door for them and people who refuse to let you do it, they want to be the door-opener, and you have a little fight about it.
People who play Boggle and people who would rather be shot in the head.
People who keep eight rolls of toilet paper in the bathroom at all times and people who call out to other people.
You like an epiphany or you like a surprise.
You are a binary thinker or you are and you aren't.
You say you basically dismantle 500 years of Western metaphysics in one fell swoop or you nap under a leaf's lip.
You think Modigliani painted nipples too small or you think Emily Carr painted trees too big.
You boil too much pasta or you don't boil enough.
You know all the different kinds of lentils or you resent your vegetarian dinner guests.

Mangoes aren't worth the hairs in your teeth or they are.
Terror of disorder keeps you up at night or terror of order does.
You have a way with animals or squirrels smell your fear and attack.
You'd like to be cremated because you believe in ethereal reincarnation rather than bodily resurrection or you'd like to be cremated just to be sure you're really dead when they put you down there.
You're not a group person or you go to political rallies and you're the first to shout 'Shame!' during the speeches.
You go to rallies because you care about the issues or you go to pick up girls.
You eat the dark meat because you prefer it or you eat the dark meat because other people want the white meat.
You think the only way to respond to a poem is to write another poem or you think the only way to respond to a poem is to run the other way.
To you, beating the system means making fake passports or beating the system means breaking the stems off the broccoli in Zehrs.
You once rescued a duck or you once bagged a buck.
Your mother put peanut butter in the gutter of your celery or she filled it with Cheez Whiz.
You are torn between the Green Party and the NDP or you are torn between the Alliance and the Christian Heritage Party. Either way, you can say both are pretty good on the gay issue.
You flex your back or you flick your Bic.
You'd like a cat in a basket or you'd like a bat in a casket.
You think you're too flat in the bazooms or too fat in the caboose.
Are you eyeing my cup of java or fucking up my vagina?
Howard Hughes ate no oranges and Allen Ginsberg ate them whole, including rind, pith and seeds.

You believe in fate and are paralyzed by the thought of your own powerlessness or you don't believe in fate and are paralyzed by indecision.

You think they don't pick up the phone because they're out of town or you think they don't pick up because they're screening and they hate you.

You need to smarten up or you need to dumb down.

You are always a bridesmaid never a bride or you are always a bride and don't have bridesmaids because you pissed off all your friends by marrying their husbands.

People think you are a good egg or a bad seed.

A free spirit or a freeloader.

You subscribe to *Gourmet* magazine or you don't want fruit in soup.

You get Gloria Steinem and Gertrude Stein mixed up or you get the Bangles and the Go-Go's mixed up.

Or Orson Welles, H. G. Wells and George Orwell.

You see an ad for a Ford SUV claiming their new folding back seat, the result of sophisticated problem-solving, 'literally lets you have your cake and eat it too' and you think *literally!?* well, they've just undermined their argument with an unsophisticated grammatical flaw and you think of calling the number at the bottom of the page – a little word to the wise – but of course you would never do such a thing, or you wouldn't do such a thing except for once when you impulsively called the RealFruit Gummies people to tell them you got a bag with no green gummies in it, telling yourself they'll want to know about flaws in production and secretly speculating that they might send you a free bag, maybe even a crate, maybe a lifetime supply of green ones, but the eighteen-year-old RealFruit Gummies customer service representative on the other end just said 'OooooоKay' like you were a complete nincompoop and now you think *Why not? I've already wasted ten minutes thinking about this, why not call Ford?* So you call and explain to the eighteen-year-old kid whose first word is 'OooooKay' that 'literally' means not figuratively and that the ad is telling us there's cake in the truck that we're having and eating, but she's not really cluing in, not really grasping the urgency of the situation, and at the end of each of your sentences you hear your own voice in her ears and know that's all she has to go on, she doesn't know how attractive and sporty and well-rounded you are and you can tell she is wondering if this is a prank call or you are a pervert or, worse – as your voice gets both thinner and more shrill, if that's possible – someone who needs to get out more.

You need to get out more or you need to get in more.

You need to branch out or you need to put down roots.

You think a pap smear involves the Vatican somehow or you have an apron that says Bar-B-Cutie on it and you wear it.

When you see a flag at half-mast you worry another former prime minister has died or you worry another Ramone has died.

You prefer the smell of chai, lavender bushes and line-dried laundry or basketballs, Magic Markers and puddles of gasoline.

You'd rather have to eat too many mini marshmallows or too much kelp.

You've fallen for a line or you've fallen for a sentence.

You are irritable or iterable.

The figurative sway of language being uncommonly effective on you, you can't eat blood oranges while you can eat candy-apple red nail polish. Or you live in Puce.

Your idea of self-discipline is to abstain from sex or your idea of self-discipline is to call yourself a naughty girl and take yourself to bed.

You think Ian Hanomansing was once husky or you think he will be husky.
You think Ian Hanomansing is the next Peter Mansbridge or you think Peter Mansbridge is the next Queen Mum.
You'd rather carve a war monument or you'd rather carve a loon.
Artillary or fritillary.
If you could turn back time, you would lock your bike or you would warn your students never to open an essay by quoting Cher.
You'd rather be thought of as dumb and actually be smart or you'd rather be thought of as smart and actually be dumb.
If you knew you'd be absolutely alone for two months, you'd never get out of the bathtub or you'd never get into the bathtub.
You talk loudly in airport lineups or you are Canadian.
You used to think honeycomb was man-made or you used to think Mt. Rushmore was a natural phenomenon.
You are in tiptop shape or you are a teapot shape.
You chose or you were born that way.
No pulp or extra pulp.
A breeze blows around you or a breeze blows through you.
You've all but given up on the perennial pursuit for contentment or you're content to find a good muffin.
You take the tunnel or you take the bridge.
You pay the toll lady or you play the lotto daily.
You like to watch the sunset or you like to watch the cliché.
You like Bits & Bites or you like Méli-Mélo.
You say 'the island' and mean Vancouver Island or you say it and mean P.E.I.
When you get a C you sink into a depression that forever scars your already tenuous sense of self-worth or you say 'All right! a C!'

You are a worrywart or you worry about your warts.

V's of geese are disturbing to you when they are asymmetrical, or when they are symmetrical.

If you could have an answer to any question about time, you'd ask whether time is indeed a Cantorian continuum or if its constitution is granular, or you would ask why is it still winter.

You jilt or you are jilted.

You tilt or you are tilted.

You think the words 'plethora' and 'penultimate' might as well be used as long as they're there or you feel it's best to just leave them be, like hotel shower caps.

Being called a nickname makes you blush and feel pleasantly confused or you fume when someone calls you Champ, Bud or H. D. Imagiste.

You feel that as you get older, your horizons expand, or you've been crossing off your options since age eleven, when you had to concede that you would never be a child chess prodigy, an Olympic gymnast or the world's shortest veterinarian.

You think Oil of Olay is for your face or you think it's for your tortilla chips.

You think you are more attractive and interesting than you are or you think you are far more attractive and interesting than you are.

When you knock over a glass you say 'Clumsy me!' or you say 'Who put that glass there?!' or you say 'Stupid cup.'

You'd rather be knee deep in interoffice memos or knee deep in slugs.

You'd rather have a swan-shaped birthmark on your face or a dimpled knee that resembles an angry Joe Clark head.

You'd send a picture of it to *Ripley's Believe it or Not* and they would believe it or not.

You could see yourself in a fake fur thong or you couldn't.
Other people could see you in a fake fur thong or they couldn't.
People could see you in a fake fur thong but wouldn't want to or they couldn't but would.
Now you want one, don't you? Or don't you.
If you were a figure in a Surrealist painting you'd be propped up or there'd be a hole through you.
You feel sorry for the mules or you feel sorry for the piano.
Linda McCartney or Heather Mills.
For you, it goes without saying or it doesn't.
In that one 'you' was really me or 'you' was really you or 'you' was Paul.
And now back to you, you would say, if you were a reporter who forgot the anchorman's name or if you were playing a very slow game of Ping Pong.
Moral DIE-lemma or moral DUH-lemma. Those who say DUH-lemma are truly having one, whereas those with DIE-lemmas put on a good show while having decided from the start to take the money or sex and run.
Your last words will be 'What is the question' or 'Hey, you're a *jumping* spider.'
If you had more time you would take a breath at commas, or you would jam more syllables in, say 'aluminium.'
If you had more time you could be a prolific writer and a long-distance runner, or an Xbox champion and compulsive masturbator.
You mark the passing of each year with a new piercing or you go to the jewellers at the mall once, at eighteen, your clammy hand shaking the jittery paw of the girl who will use the studgun for the first time. She's been taught to distract you, 'How was your summer?' she asks, punching

a needle into your right lobe. 'Great,' you say and her bracelets clink against the gun as she centres it over your left lobe. 'How was your summer?' she asks, *punch*, 'Okay,' you say.

If you could fill a time capsule to inform future generations about our culture, you would include an article on the loss of the Space Shuttle Columbia or a tape of *Entertainment Tonight* featuring Ben Affleck's response to the loss of the Space Shuttle Columbia, since he sat in it once.

You order a bidet for your kitchen because it sounds kind of classy or you say no to a Bodum because it sounds kind of dirty.

When your women's studies professor says the course will 'not be about man-hating' you feel more comfortable or you are kind of disappointed.

You are a night person or a morning person, that is if 'personhood' is defined by alertness and productivity. Perhaps 'persons' might ideally be snoozing on a full stomach in warm slanty sunshine, in a hammock or perhaps on their desk, cheek pressed to a fluorescent Post-it, in which case why not be an afternoon person.

Music and poetry are inseparable or music and poetry are insufferable.

There are two kinds of people, and one of them is Jordan Craddock, Columbus, Ohio, 1956.

When you borrow a broken pencil from someone, you sharpen it, use it and return it sharp so as to effect an even trade, or you sharpen it, use it and break it, so as to approximate the condition in which you received it.

That's what Jordan Craddock did.

It was 1956 or '57.

A pregnant lady is a treble clef or a treble clef is a snail on a fork or a snail on a fork is something French or something French is anything blue or anything blue is anything borrowed or anything borrowed is a burr in your boot or a burr in your boot is a tiny dried pufferfish stuck to your sock or a tiny dried pufferfish stuck to your sock is always a surprise and always a surprise is a pregnant lady, why is that?

Two kinds of people walk into a bar looking for a punchline, find a tedious denouement instead.

Smashing through the guardrail and plummeting to your death you shout 'I love you!' or you shout 'Fuck!'

You say 'I love you' or you say 'I love you too.'

You say 'Fuck you' or you say 'Oh yeah? Fuck you.'

And in the end the love you took is equal to the love you mook.

The medium is the message, or raisins are the reason.

You have ants in your pants or a bee in your bonnet or a luna moth in your loincloth.

You determine that there have been pickled circumstances or extenuating beets, corduroy blackouts or rolling slacks, strawberry differences or an irreconcilable tart, hat fever or a hay trick, taffy shelter or a no-kill pull, rodeo feelings or a hard clown, ceramic glances or a sidelong glaze, concrete broth or a chicken poem, reasonable mouth or mealy doubt.

Your pencil is broken or your pen is leakin' your Aunt Carla ain't Lorca or Uncle Louis isn't Catullus and fuzzy wuzzy wasn't jazzy has no knack for bugling has he taxi your artsy, or bus your bass, bust your bassoon, I stubbed my tubas!, beg Mr. Music for the cornets and the lieder or sorry hummingbird there are hornets at the feeder.

Q & A

with Nicole Markotić

Is it worth the portage? Maple or hickory-smoked? Are you serious? Which is worse? You and what army? Really? How do they expect the little guy to compete? But would they get the verdict they were looking for? What flutes? Was it malignant? How would you like an all-expenses-paid trip to sunny Cozumel, Mexico? Sugar? What version of Windows do you have? How far is Ann Arbor? You mean, like, a soft cheese? Do you like to save money? Who's a handsome mister cat? Is it Wednesday already? Air miles? Rather than the one with the pointy thing on the back of its head? Anything to declare today? A dollar thirty-nine for an avocado? What time do you close? Does she eat dairy? How long does it have to be?

Sift words into his package. My apple OR hickey OR most. You're so serious. I changed the ORs. U and I warm the real, open the how. Do your Ys X? Pecs on the little guy complete B: butter wood. The Gs Q their gaze for the sake of fluke. *What* it? Mal in *gants* how U hold. Like an L X paid for by ripping suns, co-zoos, mal-Mex and co-signs. See through the V you gave. How is Anne? Broke cheese like you like money. He's a handful, missing cat burglar weddings. *D* ain't *me*. Resolve the one with Mr. Pointy through dusty backs. Head for today, declare a dollop dirty, then fine your average day. Stymie close, whistle your shoes through dates and sheets. Long: it has to be long.

Oh, Anne's Anne. How's your moist O-ply pummelling? Fresh ground pepper, swift dints in your whisper cage? You're the serious one, pesto change-O. O and O worm the roll, owe the ooh. Do your Bees Gee? Hey, completely little guy, would you butter my pecs? OK, OK, Vs of geese. It what? Lamb on pants. Who, me? Old, like an MD I peed for, Rx: purring snooze, kazoos, cigs, sins. But do you see through the Y I gay? Cheese like you, monkey bloke. Aren't you the handful, kissing the Hamburglar's wingdings? Anoint moi. Re: O, does Mr. Tiny opt for cabs therewith? Death for a day, do a flirty poll, then refrigerate Y. Why me? It's your clothes, your whistling dishes and teats. Langue: it's langue or nothing.

O + A = A. How's your math? *Opala!* Melt freshly ground Swift into John Cage. Pepper with whistles and serious *Presto!* To change: O – O = O. Warm rolls and *Oh!* you shock the bejeezus from a list of guys. Better peek before the corral of OKs = IV. Easy, what lamb wears pants? Or whose? I like the mould, the empty racks, the purse snatching, the kangaroos. See EG: see-through sin. But why? I = guy. Sheesh, like you, I am monk; broke. R ≠ hands kissing hands. *Ring ring!* Annie's moist in Rio. Doing martinis. Top zebras force their there-withal. Date for date. Flip lopsided then refrigerate the hen. That's why. Methinks you're loath to wash dishes or line up for treats. Lastly: the thing's gotta last.

Q + A = A. Who's your moth? *Op art!* Freshet swift over Cajun ground. O whippoorwill pest! No means no means no. Oh. *Wormholes and You.* Formalists in the guise of jujubes. Beekeepers for Lorca scoff equally. Say, why blame sweat pants? Or hose? I *like* the doldrums, the empty cars, the pure snit, the aching, the angst, the blues. See eggs: these rough skins. Beauty = ugly? Shush, I'll yolk a broker. Sh, ski with Nanny's ringworm and sing, *sing!* Itsy-doozy teeny-weeny moody polka dot too windy. Tee-hee, Dada. Flop lipsided then refry Greta Henry. That's who. Mestinks; you lather. Wish for fräulein parfait. La lust: got the thing at last.

Q & A + whose mouth? Apart. Fresh, swift trobar. Can't round the whip or we'll pester the exclam. No more, no more. Woe. Horn in on the U and ə forms a list with guys and Js. Rube or rubies? Peek quickly, four times off B. Hey, he blames sweet panties? Those? Dollops of kites, carts of tempting purée, blue ants. Achoo leads to: snot. Tough gloves suggest Vs flung akimbo. Hush, we'll toke when I < broke. A husky Annie rings moist hickory around single slings. It's a tiny dozen, a wee mood, another dollop. Wind toward me: tada! Lick lips on the refrigerated side. Get the hint, that's how you tinker. Forfeit later. At 4:40? Flutes of lust, at last: lust.

ASIDE FROM

a wrong tree what is rued
the mouth what is barked up
French what is foamed at
the bird what is excused
the slip what is flipped
something fishy and a rat what is given
a long story what is smelled
my dead body what is made short
the flow what is over
your own medicine what is gone with
the eye of the beholder what is tasted
humidity what is beauty in
your head what is not heat
more than you can chew what is kept above water
a rose garden what is bitten off
an old dog what did I never promise you
the trees what cannot be taught new tricks
the dust what can one not see the forest for
the land what is bit
that bridge what did time forget
the pitch what will we cross when we come to it
the ropes what is queered
a limb what is known
the lock what is gone out on
the vote what is raped

parole what is won
the night what is he out on
the heart what is taken back
the word what is worn on sleeves
what's good for the goose what's mum's
bygones what's good for the gander
the day what are bygones let be

NEWS SUDOKU #19, LEVEL: LOWEST

Free sex on proposes vote Harper marriage same issue
Vote marriage proposes on same issue Harper sex free
Issue same Harper free sex marriage on vote proposes
Same vote issue sex free on proposes Harper marriage
On free marriage Harper proposes same sex issue vote
Harper proposes sex marriage issue vote free on same
Sex on vote issue marriage proposes same free Harper
Marriage issue free same Harper sex vote proposes on
Proposes Harper same vote on free issue marriage sex

NEWS SUDOKU #24, LEVEL:LED

A cost toll civilian half exceeds trillion million death
Trillion half million death a toll exceeds cost civilian
Civilian death exceeds cost million trillion a toll half
Half a cost million trillion civilian toll death exceeds
Toll exceeds trillion half death a million civilian cost
Million civilian death toll exceeds cost half trillion a
Cost trillion a exceeds toll death civilian half million
Death toll half a civilian million cost exceeds trillion
Exceeds million civilian trillion cost half death a toll

The one who spit.

The one who choked.

The one who drank water looking at the ceiling.

The one who drank water reading the label, with crossed eyes.

The one who unscrewed the cap of the water bottle before a poem, screwed it back on afterward, never drinking. It made us thirsty.

The one with the huge flashy earrings shaped like potato chips with bites out of them.

They made us hungry.

The one who kept calling me Sharon.

The one who kept reminding us he had been 'much anthologized' as if 'anthologized' meant 'knighted.'

The one whose entire reading consisted of standing at the podium, reading poems silently to herself, chuckling, flipping to the next one.

The one who had to have barbecue ribs 'Southern-style' and, when we finally found some, left a letter of complaint with the hotel manager because the takeout box wouldn't fit in the waste basket.

The one who said 'I'll be reading for approximately forty minutes' and then read for two hours and forty minutes, interpreting every thank-god-it's-over smattering of claps as encouragement to continue, the only exit door tantalizingly behind her, her animated head obscuring the glowing letters variously, EXI, XIT, IT, EX.

The one who was not as interesting in person.

The one we were glad to be sitting for, the story knocking the pins right out from under us.

The one we were glad to be sitting for, in case we fell asleep.

The one who always wore his 'lucky' shirt to readings, our venue the last on his three-week book tour.

The one who threw up shrimp.

The one who talked about how tedious press junkets can be, especially in Paris.

The one who needed to borrow pants.

The one who, over dinner, regaled us with hilarious anecdotes about her cat, Hawthorne, who once ate a whole can of tuna, for instance, meows when you touch his feet, and loves nothing more than twist-ties, which he'll run after if they land with a satisfying skip. And Hawthorne also loves Sundays when Grandpa, a.k.a. Gappy, comes to visit because he's always up for a good twist-tie session. When the sushi finally arrived we learned that Hawthorne would probably like it, except for the avocado and rice.

The one who thought he should be paid twice as much because of all the double entendres in his work.

The one who acted as if her success were all a terrible mistake.

The one who suffered from loud, nervous farting, especially between poems, though he capitalized, most studiously, on the camouflage of short bursts of applause.

The one who obstinately read from new work, aware we were all there to hear the greatest hits.

The one who always read final lines as if our lives
depended
on
them.

TO FEDERICO GARCÍA LORCA'S *POEMA DEL CANTE JONDO*

And After

Lost labials in
colloquial time,
evanescence.

(Soliloquy
desert left.)

The heart
front of desire,
see deviance.

(Soliloquy
desert left.)

La la, illusion of aurora
and Lesbos
advance dance.

So loquitur
desert. Tell
one undulating
desert.

–to 'Y Después'

Cave

Of craving salt
large lozenges.

(Ol cardinal
sober ol red.)

The guitar evokes
remote palsy.

(Torrential rumble
o so mysterious.)

The voice between cuts
vanishes.

(Grow alone
so bleeds red.)

Why quiver uncle
tremble in gold.

(White blanket
over your eye.)

–to 'Cueva'

Security Pass

Enter black butterflies,
fauna ache much more
june to one blank surprise
to nibble snow.

Terror deluxe
ceiling deterred.

Vacant of nothing, all tremble
done rhythm; none called
tin courage deplete
your spun~all disaster.

Wonder where
conundrum, sin, kiss?
What moon recognize
the color decal ¿alfalfa?

Turns of zeal,
its yellow error.

–to 'El Paso de la Siguiriya'

YA!

The grit in déjà vu
One solemn disciple.

(Dad and me in camp
and crying.)

Today say ah to rot in the world.
No kidding, masque the silence.

(Dad and me in camp
and crying.)

The horizontal lizard
is dead as a dog.

(Yes us dichotomous
in the camp
crying.)

–to '¡AY!'

So La La

Conman's Knee Grows Toes
pensive queue *mundane checkout*
yell core zones immense.

Invest icons too many gone.

Think suspense quote internal
yell grit, dance spare,
delve into the currency.

Vest id stomach groans.

Say hey the bacon's open
label yellow porcelain,
disembowel today local

Yabadabadoo,
gross quiver *stone* command!

–to 'La Soleá'

Notch

Circus, candle
feral lucy etiquette.

All consolation
deals état.

Vitamins of old
tumble,
that roar smacks of
crucial superstitions.

Cry Canidia,
for old lights negate.

–to 'Noche'

Falsetto

Yeah, pert'near Gitanes
!¡¡!!¡¡
Yaya pert'near.
Good girls don't
inhale ~
No no, give me more Crisco,
good guys.
(All draw a blank translating
mantillas.)
Last fairy.
Gentlemen prefer
Tsawwassen
(and *corazón* beats
heart)
in easy cab.
Quiet crying in
juice streets.
Yeah, pert'near Gitanes
!¡¡!!¡¡
Yaya pert'near.

–to 'Falseta'

My Drug Ada

Perry Como lame-o
lassos stars,
cigars

Bossy verdant notch,
tassled ass,
delirious January
clientele.

Quell la de da
more nub!¡Ada's rump
lassie jubes
filling rocks ya!
Ya! Perry Como loves
Saturdays,
stars, cigars.

–to 'Madrugada'

Silencer

Hello mojo, silent leo.
E-sun undulating coil,
unslice,
don' dress banal, be eco
inclined key front
I see a slow.

–to 'El Silencio'

Conjure

El em en o crisp
moocow Medusa
getchyer jollies doin it
nice dildel.

As is basted
just cuz us.

Sobbing human blanket
delinquent nut,
y'all go on top
and this is a primrose.

So as busted
just cuz in.

Appreciate one heart
invisible, lavish
unicorn zoo
reflected in the new tv¿

Ass¿backwards
just cuz.

–to 'Conjuro'

TRANSCRIBING THE LETTERS OF GERTRUDE STEIN AND VIRGIL THOMSON

I am practicing lejibibity, do you recognise it,
(Stein to Thomson, 23 Sept. 1928)

Thanks for the duffings.
Love to my Gody and quineff pumfally.
Smile and write look the same.
Saints and Emily.
Clippings, thanks for the clippings.
See you Tuesday. Fine, until Thursday. That's Tuesday. Yes, 'til then.
At seven in the afternoon.
After Estuary after Easter flu, full
of almost almonds.
Margaret and Nougat.
Avery Hopwood assumes or assures. Avery Hopwood amuses.
Have you been a little better? Have you sent a bitter letter?
The train comes on the hon and half-hon.
There's a good chance of having you finished
in January, or printed in Germany, printed
in January, finished in Germany.
A bitter winter. A pay official novel. Psychological.
The book was famously, permanently, persistently, furiously, permanently
lost there.
It looks like terrified hills, sewing ourselves, Alice is rippled.

It looks like buttered
nightingales, and it is.
Love to anybody and yourself pumfally.
That story about piano is rapturously narty and that story
about Picasso is xceptionally nasty.
Thanks for the Christ on Epps.

There is no famous church at Epps, there is no Epps.
Georges' 50 000 francs was so ooo famous.
Love to everybody and yourself principally.
Anyway always, smile back soon. May your mossy
grutty be revealed as snowing gently.
From an uncatalogued box, buried
in the archive, may you fish out a postcard
of the Burgos Cathedral in Spain:
Jesus standing on eggs.

GIRL WATCHING

Wow lookit her, there's a sunlit hay bale, there's a key lime pie and a million pixels.
No way, she's a mealy peach, a fourth-place finish, an overlong film clip of Stockwell Day's wetsuit.
Get out of here, she's a fresh bingo dabber, a claw-foot tub, cinnamon unwaxed floss.
Sticky kitchen floor, infected piercing, leaf blower, another Hollywood lesbian breakup.
Well how about that licorice allsort, that upbeat horoscope, roasted pine nut, team momentum, handcrafted inkwell.
Please, rental-car insurance, kitty litter dust, oldies station, warm cauliflower water, tired hams stuck to a hot vinyl car seat.
A puppy hero, a sturdy nest, nicotine patch, Fisherman's Friend, a Mt. St. Helen's floaty pen.
Lower back strain, drum machine, insufficient RAM.
She could be my waterspout, my pink paperclip, my *Hallucinogenic Toreador*.
Ugh, late bus, wet firewood, oaf cat you can't give back, favour without the 'u.'
There goes a winning ticket, slickly spinning bobbin winder.
Hockey parents, *Awake* pamphlets, fibreglass splinters, laundromat TV.
Sweet au lait, tin chimera, you're hard to pleat.
Yes, for no one is as pre-emptive as you, as spacious and choppy.
Well I'll be a silk-lined swimmer, give me a kiosk, handy rhododendron.

TSE TO SEA

(a libretto)

Very improbable structures readily arise through the cumulation of small alterations.

Selection in the diploid phase is complicated by allelic interaction.

The eyes of limpets are open cups.

Evolution makes you
crazy, doesn't it, because it renders
irrelevant ambition and desire.
You don't want to die because your hips
are too narrow. You want to be gallooned
by briary loops.
May I clone you.
A sudden blue beak,
fingers on feet, your ornamental horn.
Here are angels, patent always pending.

Replication is always imprecise.

Verily provable sutures dearly raise the rogue commutation of malls' attractions.

Elections in the Pleiades placated by alleluia in creation.

The yes of limping pets are pups.

Love's motion raised ague,
didn't it, caused the sender to be
virulent, ambient and retire.
Why don't you lie: '*boca*,' use your lips
to worry an o or two o's. Go balloon
over binary pools.
May I clone you.
A sun-baked body,
fringes on toffee, ho! mental aurora.
Hear our language, tap always ending in 'p.'

Courtship in Drosophila involves a dance in which the partners, face to face, perform a series of rapid shuffles from side to side.

Pork chop Philosopher in a candy Volvo nears the part in which, café to café, he forms a species of pied houseflies from tse to tse.

Poor chap feels safer in a revolving car park in which, coupé to coupé, he morphs special pie-eyed fleas for to see tutti.

Reptile nation swallows impresario.

Swallowing nations of pups,
wallowing passions of nups,
replicate limpets and hips,
replicate limpets and hips.
Face to face to face to face,
far too far too far too far,
far too far too far too far too far,
far too far too far too far too far
too far too far too far too far too fat.
Replicate limpets and hips,
replicate crumpets and chips,
swallowing passions and wallowing face to face,
swallowing passions and wallowing face to face.
Hydra Hydra Hydra swallowing
Hydra Hydra Hydractinia.
Leo Buss of Yale and Rick Grosberg of Davis.
Leo Buss of Yale and Rick Grosberg discovered
an example of dichotomous social behaviour,
a beautiful example of dichotomous social behaviour
in *Hydractinia*, a marine hydrozoan that forms colonies
of zooids in gastropod shells. Some genotypes are always stoloniferous.
Leo Buss of Yale and Rick Grosberg of Davis face to face.
Leo Buss of Yale and Rick Grosberg of Davis face to face.
Some genotypes are always stoloniferous; some are never stoloniferous.
Marine hydrozoan that forms colonies of zooids in gastropod shells,
the beautiful social behaviour of zooids in gastropod shells,
face to face,
dichotomous.

Tap always ending in 'p' and Patsy in tse,
pat always ending in 't' and bay always starting with 'b.'
Leo Buss of Yale.
Tap always ending in 'p' and Patsy in tse,
pat always ending in 't' and bay always starting with 'b,'
bay always ending in bee and shell always starting with 'she,'
she's always selling them shells always starting with sea.
Tse to sea to sea to sea to sea.
Tse to sea to sea to sea to sea.
She sells gastropods by the gas station.
Tse to sea to sea to sea to see two
beautiful zooids.
Tse to sea to sea to see to see to it we see it.
Tse to sea to sea to see to see to it we see it.
Pat always ending in 't,' we are clever save winter
when furry ones hibernate, winged ones migrate and skinny ones ice-skate
while winged ones migrate and furry ones hibernate, skinny ones ice-skate

in circles and
cycles and eights
and circles and beautiful
zooids and eights
and cycles and circles and
eights and circles and
cycles and
circles and all.

The principle of contingency amounts to saying that evolution is a river, not a road.

The principal of Genetic CVI says a man of education is a liver, not a load.

The prince of pathogenic VIPS names infection as a giver, not a goad.

Eerily for able poochers, early rising dogs mock mutation of rats' actions.

Technicians please play katydid, cry la la la in tune.

The synonyms of pits are pips.

Peer alienation a slow swimmer's prize.

POETSMART TRAINING FOR YOUR POET

with apologies to www.petsmart.com

Just like people, poets can develop unhealthy, unpleasant and sometimes dangerous habits. Poets are cute but, let's face it, they can disrupt a household. Like children, they need guidance and discipline to live happily and healthily with the 'adults' in their lives. From fundamental manners to problem solving, anything is possible with a good education.

POETSMART professional Poet Training Instructors can help you teach your poet a variety of skills from the basics of good behaviour to complicated tricks and everything in between. Developed by the world's leading poet trainers and behaviourists, this gentle and effective approach is fun for both poets and their families. Regardless of your poet's age or skill level, we have a course that will help him learn new desired behaviours. Choose from the following two levels:

1. Poet Head Start

Using positive reinforcement methods, you'll learn how to prevent unwanted behaviour and establish a bond with your poet. Training points include:

- House training and basic manners.
- Non-aggressive behaviour around other poets.

- Poet health care, grooming and nutrition: You can't leave hair care and oral hygiene to poets themselves! Right from the start, poets should eat in moderation and drink plenty.

- Common language and simple commands (for e.g., 'come' and 'stay,' as in 'Come with me and be my love' and 'Oh stay, three lives in one flea spare,' etc.).

- Learning to resist toys, pork chops, clichés and overwrought endings when left alone.

2. Advanced Learning Class

We'll focus on performance despite distractions, and reliability when at a distance from people. Key topics covered in these classes include:

- Performing with and without awards.

- Learning despite distractions (including everything from television to other poets in heat).

- Additional language ('heel,' 'lie down,' 'rose,' 'Ode to … ,' 'pallid,' 'marrow,' 'propinquity' and more).

- Relationship-forming games and play that maintain poet's submissive role.

- The special grooming needs of outdoor poets.
- Performance while 'off-lead' or 'free verse.'
- Quieting extreme barkers, because some poets love the sound of their own voice!

Visit a POETSMART store for more information on either of these. Don't forget to pick up treats, toys and a cozy poetbed – poets need lots of attention and some can sleep for up to 22 hours a day!

CONSTANCE ROOKE, AUTHOR OF *THE CLEAR PATH: A GUIDE TO WRITING ENGLISH ESSAYS*, AND HOME-INSPECTION CONSULTANT BRAD LABUTE CONVERSE, WITH RUDE INTERRUPTIONS BY WALT WHITMAN

There is copper, cast iron, galvanized and ABS piping in the home.
But I find this version hard to grade because it would be extremely unusual to find an essay so free of technical errors that is also so weak in argumentation.
The main water supply pipe to the home is galvanized and the shut-off valve is located in the basement.
You should not conclude, however, that the 20-percent spread between 40 percent in Version 1 and 60 percent in Version 2 represents the amount that technical errors can count in an assessment of your work.
Although galvanized piping has a life expectancy of 40 to 60 years, rust accumulates inside the pipes and chokes down the diameter.
Who goes there! Hankering, gross, mystical, nude?
Bi-metallic connections should be avoided as galvanic corrosion often occurs between pipes and fitting of different metals.
The cleaned-up copy of Version 2 makes it easier for us to see what the writer of the essay might be trying to say and how the argument can be improved.
How is it I extract strength from the beef I eat?
What is a man anyhow? What am I? and what are you?
The average life expectancy of cast iron piping is 50 years.
Notice that I have used the word 'argument' – but what *is* the argument of the essay?

That months are vacuums and the ground but wallow and filth,
That life is a suck and sell, and nothing remains at the end but threadbare crape and tears.
What is the writer trying to prove?
The flapper to the toilet on the upper level of the home stays open.
Here is what I think might have gone on in the mind of the student who submitted Version 1.
Press close barebosomed night! Press close magnetic nourishing night!
I cock my hat as I please indoors or out.
(I'll assume that the student was female.)
The roof was examined from the ground.
In reading the story, she noticed that this very old woman was doing some peculiar things – talking to shrubs, hallucinating about marble-cake, and so on.
There are three layers of asphalt shingles on the roof.
I have pried through the strata and analyzed to a hair,
As discussed on site, the shingles are generally in poor condition and there are missing shingles.
The technical carelessness of Version 1 is a symptom of the student's hurried approach to the task at hand.
Improper roof ventilation may cause attic heat build-up causing cracked, buckled or leaking shingles and leaks from water backed up under the shingles by ice dams, which are formed when snow melts and freezes at the eaves.
Mainly, it feels like plot summary.
In all people I see myself, none more and not one a barleycorn less,
And the good or bad I say of myself I say of them.

These two references are introduced by the statement that the people Pheonix meets 'denote her as inferior' – presumably because she is old, since the student goes on to say 'a grandma, granny, an old woman.'

As discussed on site, the block chimney is spalling due to the application of tar.

And I know I am solid and sound,

To me the converging objects of the universe perpetually flow,

All are written to me, and I must get what the writing means.

Can you see that 'denote' is the wrong word here?

There are no roof vents and the aluminum soffit is not vented – as discussed on site,

I wonder why the marble-cake hallucination doesn't come here (rather than in the second paragraph).

The roof venting is poor.

And I know I am deathless,

I know this orbit of mine cannot be swept by a carpenter's compass,

Another problem with paragraph unity is that

a chimney screen be installed in order to deter birds/rodents from entering the home.

I reckon I behave no prouder than the level I plant my house by after all.

Notice that the word 'rodents' is wrong. Do you see how this sentence snaps into focus if you substitute 'illusions'?

I exist as I am, that is enough,

However, as discussed on site, the wood sills are rotted and

the student hasn't given any interpretation of the dialogue

tenoned and mortised in granite,

There is some mould at the lower walls,

I laugh at what you call dissolution,
Enclosed is an information sheet on mould.
One 30-amp fuse and one 25-amp fuse in the subpanel are overrated.
My criticism of Version 2 is not so much that the essay lacks a thesis,
And I know the amplitude of time,
as that the implicit thesis is not sufficiently interesting from a literary point of view.
Unscrew the locks from the doors!
Unscrew the doors themselves from their jambs!
The S-trap should be upgraded to a P-trap.
The topic of this paragraph is love.

TWISTER

Inside now, her face pixilated by the screen door, 'You can't have your cake and eat it too!' she shouts, by way of explaining why I can't stand on the barn roof to videotape the twister and also survive it. From this vantage point the distant funnel appears to dance along the top of the clothesline T, wiggling its hips but keeping toes together. Then a roar, just like they say, and the great dark wedge is fantastic. I look side to side for wonder-confirmers, but they are all hiding their heads in cold storage so I'll have to tell them later that wind has a look, looks like grey cotton candy, the shredded batting of old insulation. And my camera is yanked, is a smear over the road, and cake wiggling, door explaining, fantastic hips and pixilated cabbages, kings wiggling its rainwater, funnelling its wheelbarrow, dark chickens distant, shredded eat it, so much toes together, hips depends upon shredded candy, on shouted wonder, a wiggling confirmer. Looks heads wedge can't way she T hips barn barn barn stand white storage byway, glazed wiggling wonder-batting, vantage batting, T and cake.

Spackling acres.
Chit.
Chit.

Marlboro flirty putts Rural Route minty pants
Bib Tip.
Tippet.

Fudgey mesh.
Shifty mussel whistle.

Bub.

Béla Bartók Béla Bartók Béla.

Is catgut really that?

Vicissitudinous. Necessitarianism. Vegetarianality.

Wonka pawpaw fop.
Cowa whipwhip poot.

At the end of the piece, not the end of the movement, that's when you can leap from chair to chair, catch claws in the velvet.

Then chit. Chit. Schedule.

Now swat smitten.

Wit.

Nap.

Piccolos.

A croissant
filled with
piping hot mice.

UNFILLED PRESCRIPTION

Difficulty is
hard.

Unbucked up, walk-
ing as if

moving, boots-
traps tucked.

Birds chin up,
drill.

Love
cupped
around a glint.

WHO WILL MAKE THE TEARS WET FOR THE FIRST TIME IN ENGLISH LITERATURE IN 200 YEARS?

Your tears will have to bubble out of faces, they'll have to shoot out like hard seeds, they'll have to fly up rather than fall, hit the ceiling but not ricochet down (they can't go down anymore). They'll bore right through the roof and hit geese in the stomach, *squawnk*. The tears themselves will have to *squawnk* or make the sound of a sleeping-bag zipper. They'll have to taste like rusty bolts or coconut pudding. They'll have to be double drops, Siamese twin drops, bobbly upside-down hearts that are indecisive about which way to stream, jig this way and that like little dancing bums. Then I'll feel sorry for you. Jessica watched her grandmother board the plane, and tears welled up in her navel. Walking back through the airport, people stared at the wet spot and she knew what it was to be a Teletubby. He took my hand at the altar and his eyes shone and he puked. I started to spew too, and everyone around us said 'Aw,' a few of them wiping drool away with tissues. She was self-conscious about her smelly tears but, dammit, sometimes you had to just let 'em rip. Cry me a liver, baby – raw, glistening clot or pan-fried with onion strips – either way, I'll never lick your face again. At 9:02 on a Monday morning, Sarah's bundle of joy arrived, and everybody in the room squirted tears so enormous they had to dab at their faces with diapers. The doctor couldn't see through his own deluge and croaked simply, 'It's a baby!', the nurses holding a bucket under his chin. The ranchhand was wracked with dry sobs, wept ribbons of sand onto the slick hide of the stillborn calf. Hold them back, brush them aside. It's the allergies, turn away, good idea.

TEXTBOOK CASE:

QUESTIONS TO CONSIDER REGARDING OUR LAST PHONE CALL

1. What was the conflict driving the conversation? Can you state it in one sentence?

2. You said, 'Can't live with you, can't live without you.' Was that an instance of irony, paradox or cliché? Explain.

3. Metaphors contribute colour and complexity to language use. For example, while every human being *has* an asshole, one can't literally *be* an asshole, yet the word was used as if this were so. How did this metaphor add to the conversation?

4. How did our conversation differ from Eugene O'Neill's *Long Day's Journey into Night*? How was it the same?

5. What would we lose if we were to paraphrase the conversation?

6. What do you think you meant by 'I'd prefer not to see you anymore'? What characteristics might you have in common with Melville's Bartleby?

7. How did you feel when the main character, me, fell silent? What do you think I was thinking?

8. How did punctuation affect the overall meaning of the conversation?

9. One way to view this conversation is as a lovers' spat. How might this be appropriate? How might the conversation be seen as more serious than this?

10. Note the use of 'mustard' and 'bastard.' Why did I use a half-rhyme (or 'slant rhyme') there?

11. Do you think I will forgive you? Cite evidence from the conversation to support your answer.

12. Which one of us would be most usefully defined using Miller's concept of tragic heroism? Explain.

13. What was the role of the 'goat-footed / balloonMan' in the conversation?

14. One of the moral questions addressed in our conversation is this: Which is more damaging to the spirit, deception of others or self-deception? Well?

15. Recall your closing speech. Was this dialogue or soliloquy? Explain. To me.

16. Choose a character from *The Glass Menagerie*. Was I such a bad girlfriend after all?

Left: Trace pictograph of an elk in the fine veins of your temple. Right: If it were a Virgin Mary we'd be on the news. Left: Try to sit you up for a burp, you're still latched on. Right: Milk drops leave shiny slug trails across your cheek. Left: Reading at the same time, my book on your hip, worried the officious prose style will come through in the milk, give you gas. Right: Doping for sleep. Left: Feeling like a mother didn't happen when you were born, or when I first fed you, or first used the word 'daughter.' It's happening six months later, in the dark, as a mosquito kazoos around and, without a second's hesitation, I pull up your covers, lay my bare arms on top of the blanket, whisper 'bite me.' Right: I wasn't talking to you. Left: Too tired to look at the clock, come under here, little bug. Right: Why is an elk worth nothing but a Virgin Mary on grilled cheese costs $28,000? Left: Hand straight up in the air like a flamenco dancer, articulate fingers. Right: *I've seen parents put their infants to bed right after eating, often because the baby falls asleep on the breast or bottle. I don't advise this for two reasons.* Left: Grinning kitten races off with the breast-pad Frisbee. Right: *One, the baby becomes dependent on the bottle or breast, and soon needs it to fall asleep. Two, do YOU want to sleep after every meal?* Left: Actually, yes. Right: The TV flashes against your cheek, a small smooth screen. Left: Through the blinds, moonlight strips stratify the bars of your crib. Right: From down here on the futon I watch your mobile. Left: The green bunny's coming around again. Right: Sun's coming up please don't notice. Left: You spit up to make room for more, like the Romans. Right: I wipe grains of sweat from your brow, as if you were a doctor delivering a baby. Left: October and the low afternoon sun glows through your jack-o'-lantern ears. Right: Richard's brought Chinese food, hot grease silhouettes on the paper bags, put-puttering from your diaper, does he know it's you? Left: I wish I had a suit with feet. Right: Puddin'. Left: Ruby jujube. Right: When was the last time I hummed and glugged simultaneously? Left: Not again. Right: From this angle the window that looks onto the pear trees instead looks up beyond them, incessant blue jays heading south, crossing the paler blue square of sky in groups of seven, five, nine, seven, five, as if on a loop, going and going and we two are warm enough and staying. Left: I drink milk at the same time: Am I an elaborate step that could be skipped? Right: Little lambs caper on the flannel blanket, twist one up and clean out your earhole with it. Left: Before writing a poem about it I sometimes forgot, repeated sides. Right: Three years ago in Texas, Peruvian immigrants had their children taken away when the photo-shop clerk developed their breastfeeding pictures and called the cops; a nipple in a baby's mouth was a second-degree felony, 'Sexual performance of a minor.' Left: I close my eyes, these days getting only the kind of sleep you have on planes. Right: *Extracting oil from Alberta's tar sands requires three barrels of water for each barrel of oil produced.* Left: Heave you over my shoulder, pink terrycloth sack of cream. Right: Your 'wrist' is a crease circling your fat arm like a too-tight string. Left: Still pitch before dawn and while you eat I dream a little, that you were born a gnome, and I loved you just as much, maybe more. Right: Dimples for knuckles. Left: Dark green eye keeps darting up at me, as if finally putting the face and the food together. Right: I wouldn't write this poem in Texas. Left: I never wanted to be one of those grown women with a teddy bear room. Right: *Passion is injurious to the mother's milk, and consequently to the child. Sudden joy and grief frequently disorder the infant's bowels, producing griping, looseness, etc.* Left: Now that you've started solids, applesauce in your eyebrows, I've become a course. Right: Spider on the plastic space mobile, walking the perimeter of the yellow crescent moon. Left: Dollop. Right: Now it's on Saturn's rings; if it fell off it would drop right into my mouth. Left: I take 2%, you take hindmilk. Right: Fingers shrimp their way through the afghan holes. Left: I have *hindmilk*. Right: We watch the show about you, the young and the restless. You keep smacking your lips off and craning your neck back to see what the devil Victor's on about now. Left: Beads of milk pop out before your mouth even gets there. Right: What if your donor turned out to be Eric Braeden, who plays the patriarch Victor Newman, what if you concluded every one of our disagreements with a curt and authoritative 'End of discussion.' Left: Heat gusts through the vent, stirs stars. Right: This little piggy had tofu wieners, this little piggy had none. Left: Ugh, plugged ducts. Right: How did the childless author of *Tender Buttons* know? Left: I can't move to change the station from the man who keeps saying 'As far as the weather ... ' without adding 'goes' or 'is concerned.' Right: You've got it made as far as milk. Left: Your lashes fall to your cheeks, the tiny nail clippers are within reach, and I plan the great triumph of my afternoon. Right: Kitten licks your head, leaves welts. Left: I could go for a fontanelle about now. Right: *He was put in a pie by Mrs. McGregor.* Left: Lying down together, your foreshortened head huge, I remember your birth. Right: The other side always lets down, twins the default setting. Left: You smile at a private joke, milk floods out the corners. Right: One for the road. Left: In the bathroom at the Woodstock service station a changing table, and thank goodness a small metal chair, which I would never have noticed before you came, or if I did would have thought it an odd luxury, for doing up boots or taking a load off. Right: In a different house, you keep a watchful eye, dark magnetic northern lake. Left: Feet curl in your shrunk sleeper, grandma says you'll get bunions. Right: You wet your suit, and mine, while drinking, like a functional doll I once had, her innards a single fine plastic tube. Left: The other grandma said you'll be bowlegged if we stand you up too much. Right: Their hardcover *Oryx and Crake* is too heavy so I read a musty pamphlet my mother got when pregnant with me: *Girls will feel dowdy at this time, so wearing heels can give their spirits an extra boost.* Left: You latch on to my elbow and I'm surprised, as if I'd imagined you can see in the dark, forgetting you too are only human. Right: No longer eating, you keep lips latched, flutter your tongue, tender moth or creepy guy. Left: I thought she said 'History in the *milking*.' Right: It's easier to pinch the skin of older mothers. Left: I don't know Elmo let alone Baby Elmo. Right: Your nostrils are wheels on a tiny pink VW Beetle. Left: The doctor says you have thrush – I don't have my baby-care guide, but here's a *Peterson Field Guide* which says you should have a conspicuous eyering, a distinctly orange cast about the head, ghostlike spots, legs more dusky than your toes, your voice a melodic flutelike rolling from high to low to high, *whee-toolee-weee*, and you are presumed to winter in the hills of Hispaniola. Right: Wing, whale, to-lifer, to-know, to-die. Left: Wing, ward, overs, most, -ism. Right: Stuff, side up, on, of way, of search, of asylum. Left: Bunny rattle nestled in the crook of your arm, your entire arm nestled in the crook of my hand. Right: Insert scenes of battle for more universal appeal. Left: You would win a nestling tournament. Right: No chair in the westbound service station, so we nurse in the bathroom stall, the diaper bag too heavy for the coat hook and it ticks and falters then smacks at my feet – you don't miss a swallow. Left: Here is the baby-care guide, which says I can catch thrush from you and could experience red, itchy, cracked and burning nipples and shooting pains while nursing. Finally, the kind of *mammaire verité* and deromanticization of motherhood the reader expected. Right: *See the way new trees flourish when they get started on a nurse log. Also called a mother stump, nurse logs are trees that have fallen and started to rot.* Left: Your Fisher-Price crib aquarium emits enough light to nurse by, enough surf sound to imagine myself in a hammock under coconut palms, a crab on my nipple. Right: If we've already established that you're a star why would we wonder what you are? Left: Just when I was being a smart aleck about deromanticization, a sharp tooth. Right: I guess it's like, star, what are you, *really*. Left: Geese shouting *hockey hockey hockey*. Right: I thought I was supposed to be the one cheek-pinching and chin-chucking. Left: You talk with your mouth full and wear your hat to the table. Right: Snow. Last November I didn't see it, had the calendar turned to May, waiting for you to see your first everything. Left: Your first words emerging, you shout *Hi!* to my chest before latching on, *Meow!* when you're done. Right: Teddy Graham crumbs in my $40 bra. Left: Unlike the cat, whose paws twitch while he dreams of chasing, you dream you are doing precisely what you are doing. Right: It's referred to as 'letting down,' although you feel the opposite. Left: Handed, fielder, brain, Bank, atrioventricular valve. Right: Minded, -ism, handed, ful, fielder, face, circular cone, brain, Bank, away, ascension. Left: Skim-milk light through the curtain, it must have snowed in the night. Right: Cat eating plastic, just out of reach. Left: So these are 'jugs.' Right: *A good nurse is judicious, and obeys the medical man's orders to the very letter, while, on the other hand, a bad nurse acts on her own judgement, and is always quacking, interfering and fussing with the breast. Such conceited, meddlesome nurses are to be studiously avoided; they often cause, from their meddlesome ways, the breasts to gather.* Left: Lift. Right: Tuft. Left: Loved. Right: Lift her. Left: Richter. Lift her wrote her wrought her daughter laughter lifter sitter safe her light left on her. Right: Snowbound and out of milk. I could express into my tea, but I'm not making yogourt. Left: On the other temple, veins outline a house, a single plume of smoke threading up into your hair, a bare tree in the front yard. Right: Dress you in a lamb suit in the hopes your babysitter will be tender with you. Left: One more nurse before I leave, Heidi still wearing earrings, a clean sweater, a game expression. Right: Ouch, there's the other tooth you cut this evening, kicking and clawing at Heidi with the labour of it, was the bottle of Amarula thanks enough, while we went to a party where adults conversed about who would win the federal election after the Gomery report, and if you had to sleep with a man who would it be, and we razzed the hosts about their carefully worded invitation: 'We hope that you will be able to find a sitter and join us,' Heidi at that moment bouncing the hollering lamb and trying to open applesauce with one hand, Johnny Depp won a majority, I know objectively speaking the cappuccino crème brûlée was delicious but I couldn't taste it for missing you. Left: Home again late, you're fed at 2 a.m. without having to ask and you gurgle proudly as if I've finally caught on. Right: You thump your palm on my chest, then your own, you and me, I agree, difficult to distinguish. Left: Tethered to you, I must postpone killing that spider, forced to witness her labour, empathize with her line-by-line desires. Right: My left, your right. Left: Today I fed peaches to someone who's never heard of peaches. Ditto the moon, every Christmas carol, horse and the word 'horse.' Right: I used to need two hands and a nursing pillow, now I can erase the hell out of two sudokus, you outside the halo of the booklight. Left: 2 or a 6, 2 or a 6, 2 or a 6 or a 7. Right: This is expressive verse. Left: You pause to swish milk between your gums – a bit oaky this morning, a bit sassy, a bit maternal. Right: House finch below the feeder, raspberry throat among a party of sparrows, you hang back embarrassed to be the only one who dressed up, I think you look good. Left: Check later to see if 'snorfle' is a word. Right: Tufted titmouse, who is neither, nor is it all that tufty. Left: The closest thing was 'snorkel' which is kind of the opposite. Right: Emerging teeth like white stitches glowing in your gums. Left: In fact, you are more of a tufted titmouse than that bird was. Right: You kick through your snaps, hoist a foot into the icy dark. Left: I must have heard you crying, awakened, stood up, leant over the crib to ply the binky and the fuzzy sheep, sung 'Baby's Boat' to no avail, given in, picked you up, careful not to knock your head against the mobile, dug amongst your books for the mat to put on the futon, laid you down, unbuttoned my shirt, unhooked the nursing bra, found your mouth, because here we are but I don't remember the last ten minutes on the road. Right: I can never rest now, knowing the teeth are there, like a gun in a play. Left: a noisy slurping emanates from our airport bathroom stall, *Last call flight 142 to Calgary*, you pretend not to hear. Right: They suggested nursing for takeoff to save baby's tender ears, *that* you heard, and you milk it all the way across two Great Lakes. Left: The extravagantly indecisive route of the river through the prairie, ribbon candy. Right: Little cherub, clouds about your head. Left: Wishing that kid in front would put a sock in it. Right: Grandma K's house full of mirrors and you are jealous of all the other nursing babies. Left: The line along the elk's neck ruff extends down further than I had first noticed, leg bent elegantly above your ear. Right: A new place, and you are too excited to sleep. Left: Here three can fit in the king-sized bed and you keep shimmying down to make an H of us. Right: You are no longer an infant, not yet a toddler, just a plain old baby. Left: Are you a tot? What is the age range of tots? Right: In the Mothers' Room at the Calgary Zoo, your feet are the biggest, your burp the most robust, and I can see the other mothers doubt my claim that you are only six months old, think perhaps I have either lost my mind a little or stolen you. Left: You place your palm on my cheek and guide me away from the adult conversation, back to the appropriate downward, adoring gaze. Right: *If he be suckled after he be twelve months old, he is generally pale, flabby, unhealthy and rickety; and the mother is usually nervous, emaciated and hysterical.* Left: You've got a hold on the right, like a chain smoker. Right: The days are shorter, the curtains heavier, and we seem always to be nursing in the dark, mistaking eyes for mouths, wrist bones for nipples. Left: Pet your felt head, to keep you awake and on task. Right: Lambie. Left: Eyeing my inflating belly, friends would ask 'You're not going to start writing sentimental mothering poems are you?' Right: The mirrors distract both of us; why did I think I could cut my own hair? Left: We park to eat lunch with a breathtaking Kananaskis view, you fascinated by the Mr. Lube sticker. Right: I'm no athlete but I could pitch for La Leche League. Left: All soft-skin similes would have nowhere to go but right back to you. Right: Imprint of my sweatshirt zipper across your chin, Frankenstein's baby. Left: You thrash around in your sleeper until one leg flaps flat and the other is packed with knees. Right: The red numbers on the digital clock are huge, like in your birthing room or a train station. Left: At 3:51 I realize I could spell your name on a calculator. Right: The more you drink, the more chance you'll wet Grandma's guest bed. Left: If the goods flow one way, why are we both 'nursing'? Right: You're not really hungry, just social drinking. Left: The prairie climate is dry and your nose clogs, you resent having to pause for jagged gasps of air like you're trying to win a swimming race. Right: Nursing you for the sixth time in as many hours, eyelids puffed between open and closed, I hear a butter knife scuff toast and clang in the marmalade jar and someone asking 'Are they *still* sleeping?' Left: Warily you relinquish your stuffed mouse, so that airport security can check it for bombs. Right: How to hide my breast without smothering you as the gay steward offers me mini pretzels.

Left: They put us all in the parents' ghetto – across the aisle, *two* babies with *one* mum. Right: Your smells make us embarrassed and sorry for the people around us until we hear the group ahead is visiting Ontario to hunt. Left: Home, and you are too excited to sleep. Right: You pat my belly, the old stomping grounds. Left: The plastic moon glints in the light of the real moon. Right: Joy is so exhausting.

ACKNOWLEDGEMENTS

I am grateful for the abiding inspiration, collaboration and support of writers Nicole Markotić, Heidi Jacobs, Louis Cabri, Alan Sears, Meredith and Peter Quartermain, Margaret Christakos, Tom Dilworth, Fred Wah and Pauline Butling, and all the students in my creative writing workshops at the University of Windsor. I thank my friends and family, especially Lori and Elise, for love and indulgence. Thanks to Graham Law for the beautiful cover photo. My Coach House heroes are Alana Wilcox, Evan Munday, Christina Palassio and my wise and generous editor, Kevin Connolly.

Poems from this manuscript have previously appeared in the journals *Rampike*, *The Walrus*, *Open Letter*, *filling Station*, *dANDelion*, *Prairie Fire*, *W*, *West Coast Line*, *The Literary Review of Canada* and in the anthologies *White Ink*, *Re:Generations: Canadian Women Poets in Converstion*, *Not for Mothers Only* and *Prismatic Publics: Innovative Canadian Women's Poetry and Poetics*.

'Good Egg Bad Seed' was first published by Meredith and Peter Quartermain as a Nomados chapbook in 2004.

Phrases have been pilfered, spliced and transcreated from a range of texts, from Pye Chavasse's *Advice to a Wife on the Management of Her Own Health* to the insert from a Tampax box, from Oscar Wilde's *Salome* to a textbook on evolution, Graham Bell's *The Basics of Selection*. I stole most extensively and brazenly from Constance Rooke (*The Clear Path: A Guide to Writing English Essays*), Walt Whitman (*Leaves of Grass*) and Brad LaBute (the inspection report on our house); I thank them for material that is useful, beautiful and imperative, respectively.

ABOUT THE AUTHOR

Susan Holbrook is a poet and fiction writer whose first book, *misled*, was shortlisted for the Pat Lowther Memorial Award and the Stephen J. Stephensson Award. Her chapbook *Good Egg Bad Seed* was published by Nomados in 2004. She teaches North American literatures and creative writing at the University of Windsor. She recently co-edited *The Letters of Gertrude Stein and Virgil Thomson: Composition as Conversation* (Oxford University Press, 2009).

Typeset in Sabon Next
Printed and bound at the Coach House on bpNichol Lane, 2009

Edited by Kevin Connolly
Designed by Alana Wilcox
Cover photograph, *Iggy, c/u*, by Graham Law, courtesy of the artist (glaw.com)

Coach House Books
401 Huron Street on bpNichol Lane
Toronto ON M5S 2G5

416 979 2217
800 367 6360

mail@chbooks.com
www.chbooks.com